In his book *King*[illegible]
a refreshing and c[illegible]
God and how it is to be manifested "on earth as it is in heaven." His clarion call for Christ followers to live as expressions of that kingdom through lifestyles of love and holiness in the name of Christ is much needed in today's culture of tolerance and compromise. This book is both scripturally sound and practical in application.

— **Randy Cordell**, Lead Pastor, Lakeshore Christian Church, Nashville, TN

This book is a very precise and focused illumination on two aspects of God's character that are critical to the kingdom of God. It offers the reader insight into God's holiness and God's love in a way that brings out practically how we promote the kingdom of God. The kingdom is empowered by this read.

— **Alvin L. Daniels**, Minister, Hope Church of Christ, Miami, FL

I can't think of a more important subject. In this angry, reactive, and self-centered world, we must strive for holiness and a cross-shaped love to reveal God's kingdom and Christ the King. I'm excited about the enrichment this book will bring to all people.

— **Dr. Michael C. Turner**, President, Amridge University

Dr. Teamer offers a thoroughly biblical and practical paradigm shift on the subject of the kingdom. He challenges us to do more than name-drop the kingdom for identity's sake and to instead reflect the behavior and values of God's authoritative rule. A truly informational, inspirational, and impactful work.

— **David Wilson**, Minister, Kings Church of Christ, Brooklyn, NY

Alondra,
May God bless you
in+on your Kingdom journey!

9

KINGDOM LIFE

EXPERIENCING GOD'S REIGN THROUGH LOVE AND HOLINESS

KELVIN TEAMER

RENEW.org

Kingdom Life: Experiencing God's Reign Through Love and Holiness

Requests for information should be sent via e-mail to Renew. Visit Renew.org for contact information.

Italics have been added to Scripture quotations by the author.

ISBN (paperback) 978-1-949921-69-4
ISBN (Mobi) 978-1-949921-70-0
ISBN (ePub) 978-1-949921-71-7

Cover and interior design by Harrington Interactive Media (harringtoninteractive.com)

Printed in the United States of America

To Kim . . . you are my love and my inspiration.
To Joshua and Jordan . . . "Whatever it takes!"

CONTENTS

GENERAL EDITORS' NOTE

Jesus talked more about the kingdom of God than any other topic. After his resurrection, and before he ascended to heaven, the kingdom was the focus of what Jesus taught his disciples (Acts 1:3). It is important for disciples of Jesus to understand the kingdom.

Kelvin Teamer is uniquely suited to teach us about the kingdom. Kelvin serves as the evangelist of the Church of Christ at Bouldercrest in Atlanta, Georgia. Kelvin has earned degrees from Southern Illinois University, Georgia School of Preaching and Biblical Studies, and Amridge University (MDiv and DMin). He also serves as Adjunct Professor of Theology at Amridge University. Kelvin has been married to Kim for the past twenty-three years, and they have two children, Joshua and Jordan.

This book expounds on the section from the Renew.org Leaders' Faith Statement called "Kingdom Life":

> We believe in the present kingdom reign of God, the power of the Holy Spirit to transform people, and the priority of the local church. God's holiness should lead our churches to reject lifestyles characterized by pride, sexual immorality, homosexuality, easy divorce, idolatry, greed, materialism, gossip, slander, racism, violence, and the like. God's love should lead our churches to emphasize love as the distinguishing sign of a true disciple. Love for one another should make the church like an extended family—a fellowship of married people, singles, elderly, and children who are all brothers and sisters to one another. The love of the extended church family to one another is vitally important. Love should be expressed in both service to the church and to the surrounding community. It leads to the breaking down of walls (racial, social, political), evangelism, acts of mercy, compassion, forgiveness, and the like. By demonstrating the ways of Jesus, the church reveals God's kingdom reign to the watching world.

*See the full Network Faith Statements at the end of this book.

Support Scriptures: 1 Corinthians 1:2; Galatians 5:19–21; Ephesians 5:3–7; Colossians 3:5–9; Matthew 19:3–12; Romans 1:26–32; 14:17–18; 1 Peter 1:15–16; Matthew 25:31–46; John 13:34–35; Colossians 3:12–13; 1 John 3:16; 1 Corinthians 13:1–13; 2 Corinthians 5:16–21.

The following tips might help you use this book more effectively (and the other books in the *Real Life Theology* series):

1. *Five questions, answers, and Scriptures.* We framed this book around five key questions with five short answers and five notable Scriptures. This format provides clarity, making it easier to commit crucial information to memory. This format also enables the books in the *Real Life Theology* series to support our catechism. Our catechism is a series of fixed questions and answers for instruction in church or home. In all, the series has fifty-two questions, answers, and key Scriptures. This particular book focuses on the five that are most pertinent to kingdom living.

2. *Personal reflection.* At the end of each chapter are six reflection questions. Each chapter is short and intended for everyday people to read and then process. The questions help you to engage the specific teachings and, if you prefer, to journal your practical reflections.
3. *Discussion questions.* The reflection questions double as discussion-group questions. Even if you do not write down the answers, the questions can be used to stimulate group conversation.
4. *Summary videos.* You can find three to seven-minute video teachings that summarize the book, as well as each chapter, at Renew.org. These short videos can function as standalone teachings. But for groups or group leaders using the book, they can also be used to launch discussion of the reading.

May God use this book to fuel faithful and effective disciple making in your life and church.

For King Jesus,
Bobby Harrington and Daniel McCoy
General Editors, *Real Life Theology* Series

INTRODUCTION

On May 19, 2018, numerous people in the United States awakened from their slumber to witness what many believed to be the "wedding of the year." Such is usually the moniker given to any would-be "royal wedding." Although the US has no official ties to the British monarchy, Americans (whether or not they admit it) seem to be fascinated with the activities of the royal family of Queen Elizabeth, Prince Charles, and the late Princess Diana. On this day in 2018, Prince Harry, the youngest of the Charles and Diana brood, was set to wed American actress Meghan Markle.

Meghan Markle to Americans is no ordinary bride. She is one of ours and at the time was going to become part of the British royal family. She would emerge a *princess (a duchess to be exact)*, and the intrigue of that to those bearing witness was palpable.

In the weeks leading up to the wedding, many British traditionalists resisted the marriage, taking issue with Harry marrying an American, not to mention one who had African-American genes. Little did anyone know at the time that this resistance (which the couple would later allege was racially based) would eventually become a factor in why they left the very realm that intrigues so many of us.

Being in the British royal family brings great scrutiny and attention, not to mention its strict traditions, guidelines, rules, and responsibilities that come with the kingdom life. For Meghan to move from a career in acting into the family of a ruling monarch involved a sacrifice and surrender of all that she was used to in order for her to "take" to a new kingdom. To do this, she would have to move from a do-it-yourself, American self-rule, to being ruled by the guidelines of another kingdom. The Duke and Duchess of Sussex felt the pressure to break away from that kingdom.

Less than two years following their celebrated wedding, Harry and Meghan announced that they were opting out of their duties as senior royals to live a more independent life. One could not blame them. And it isn't my goal to take a stance on this or disparage this couple, nor any other parties involved, including the Queen of England. My goal is to highlight the fact that not everyone "takes" to the kingdom life. Many, if given the choice, would choose something else for their lives: something more independent, something freer.

We all want freedom. People have sacrificed their lives for the thought and hope of freedom, whether that freedom was from foreign oppressors or from the Jim Crow despotism in America. Freedom is a treasured value. Surrendering to the life of a kingdom rarely brings the freedom that people crave.

But what if you could have both? What if freedom and surrender could be simultaneously experienced? What if freedom could be enjoyed underneath the rule of another? What if there were a way to have that type of heaven here on earth?

> **WHAT IF FREEDOM AND SURRENDER COULD BE SIMULTANEOUSLY EXPERIENCED?**

I want to propose a way to have that and a lot more. There is an existing kingdom that offers freedom, joy, peace, love, and hope. It is ruled by a king who is just and honorable and even perfect.

To experience this kingdom, however, we must surrender our own kingdom, our own freedom, and our own rule. The result? We get to enjoy a freedom that is so much greater than anything a kingdom of self-rule could possibly bring us. This kingdom is the kingdom of God. The king whom I am speaking about is King Jesus. The life I want to reveal in this book is kingdom life.

This life will ask everything of you, but it promises to replace everything you have given up with something better, more precious, and more valuable. This is available to all people. Now, when we leave, our old kingdom offers resistance to the new rule. Like a foreign kidney struggles in an unnatural host, your body will seek to reject it, but if it "takes," your future will be much better than your past. And, truthfully, it is vital that it "takes." It is God's fervent hope that we surrender to this new rule.

I believe our life within God's kingdom begins by understanding what the kingdom life is all about. If you are keenly interested in living this way, I invite you to read on. Each of us has a life to lose, but everything to gain. When we join it, we do it all for King Jesus! So to Harry, Meghan, and anyone else seeking freedom, I introduce you to the great kingdom of God. I present to you *Kingdom Life.*

1

WHAT IS THE KINGDOM OF GOD?

***Answer:** The kingdom of God is the realm where God's will is being done on earth as it is in heaven through the reign of King Jesus.*

But seek first his kingdom and his righteousness, and all these things will be given to you as well.
— Matthew 6:33

For me, high school was tough. I had been a "big man on campus" during my junior high years, but then, all of a sudden, I was thrust into a new environment with so many more new people and a boatload of new classes. Socially and academically, I felt like everyone was moving at a different speed than I was. High school . . . I just didn't get it.

A microcosm of my high school experience was Algebra 1. For years, before this class began, I had been taught real-life numbers, but then I was transported into a world of integers, x's, y's, and square roots. Everyone around me seemed to understand this mathematical foreign language except for me. I just didn't get it.

My *not* understanding it was problematic because I was told that I would need to learn this form of math to "get through life." So, I tried to buckle down. I stayed after class, came to school early, got tutors, and hoped that I would finally understand. My efforts didn't work. I still just didn't get it.

Now before this point, my default excuse when I struggled in school had been to blame the teacher. It *had to* be their fault that I didn't understand what they were teaching, but this time I realized it wasn't because of them. It was all on me. I didn't get it because it was hard for me to see a world through anything other than what I had been used to.

I didn't adjust well to high school in general because I had been too used to elementary and middle school. And I didn't get Algebra 1 because I was too used to "regular math." Things finally began to change for me, however, when I allowed myself to put down my expectations and move away from what I had been used to. Once I approached Algebra with a sense of discovery, things began to click, and my grades began to improve—all because I opened myself up to something new!

SOMETHING NEW

SOMETHING NEW WAS WHAT the kingdom of God would have represented to those of Jesus' day, and it represents the same for us today. As such, I find that people often approach any talk of the kingdom in the same way I approached Algebra 1 early on—they have trouble understanding it.

While many of today's biblical scholars commonly hold that Jesus spoke about the kingdom of God more than anything else, as the editors of this series mentioned in the introduction, I don't think the church at large realizes it. More than love, heaven, or the church, Jesus spoke about the kingdom of God. Jesus came to earth because of the kingdom of God (John 18:37).

Since this is the case, how did this deficiency in the church's teaching happen?

MORE THAN LOVE, HEAVEN, OR THE CHURCH, JESUS SPOKE ABOUT THE KINGDOM OF GOD.

Now, I was raised in the church. My dad was an evangelist who helped plant two churches in Illinois. Yet throughout my childhood and into my adulthood, I never heard anything besides a passing remark about the kingdom of God. When I heard about it, people used the term "synonymously" with the "church," not some grand kingdom of the God of heaven and earth! For me, the kingdom of God was a muted reference, at best. I believe for many people, it still is, and because of such, the kingdom of God is often viewed as a complicated concept.

But think about it: Would Jesus spend more than three years on this earth preaching about something that was too complicated to understand? I think not. Why are we missing the importance of Jesus' message of the kingdom? Maybe we're missing the significance of the kingdom because we are not used to seeing it as anything beyond the functions of the church. And if we don't understand the kingdom of God, how can we expect for the kingdom life to "take" within the lives we've already built?

So let's try to understand the kingdom by defining it. To do so will require us to immerse ourselves in Scripture, for there we find the kingdom of God described and the kingdom life exemplified. The kingdom of God is a supremely biblical concept, and Scripture unveils its nature through the unfolding of the biblical record. The kingdom spans the Old and New Testaments. It is found in the stories of Adam, Abraham, David, Jesus, Peter, and Paul. It is seen in Israel and the church. The kingdom is here and yet it is coming. It is complex yet surprisingly simple.

WHAT IS THE KINGDOM?

The common Hebrew word used in the Old Testament for kingdom is *mamlāḵâ*, meaning "dominion" or "sovereignty." The Greek word for "kingdom" used in the New Testament is *basileia*, which is typically defined as "reign" or "rule." The kingdom of God in both these biblical languages, in its most basic sense, means *the reign and rule of God*. It is the space in which God has dominion. It is where God rules as king. Knowing this basic definition, however, only takes us so far. One must *see* it in practice in order *to* practice it.

THE GENESIS OF THE KINGDOM

The kingdom of God is birthed in the creation story. The picture of Adam, Eve, and the garden are a microcosmic foreshadowing of the kingdom. As we imaginatively venture into the majestic garden, planted by God himself, we see everything that is good—a wonderful image of the kingdom.

We know from Genesis that man and woman were formed and shaped by God and given the task to work, tend, and rule creation for God. While they were to rule over the garden *for* him, it was God who truly ruled. Everything was the way he designed it to be. *His will had been done on earth as it was in heaven.* I want you to breathe in that last statement and its context. *God's will being done on earth as it is in heaven* is a key point in understanding (and even witnessing) what the kingdom looks like, for it is what the very reign of God produces.

HIS WILL HAD BEEN DONE ON EARTH AS IT WAS IN HEAVEN.

THE KINGDOM OF GOD IN THE OLD TESTAMENT

AUTHOR AND MINISTER DAVID Young wrote, "The Old Testament was written so that we could understand what the kingdom of God is."[1] I agree. From Eden to Abraham, from Moses to David, from Isaiah to Malachi, we come face-to-face with the kingdom of God.

Scholar Scot McKnight professes that the biblical idea of the kingdom is deeply rooted in the Old

Testament Scriptures and is grounded in the confidence that there is one eternal, living God who has revealed himself to us and who has a purpose for the human race, which he chose to accomplish through Israel.[2] After Eden, it is to the ancient people of Abraham, Isaac, and Jacob that we will look to understand the kingdom of God.

> Now the LORD said to Abram, "Go from your country and your kindred and your father's house to the land that I will show you. And I will make of you a great nation, and I will bless you and make your name great, so that you will be a blessing. I will bless those who bless you, and him who dishonors you I will curse, and in you all the families of the earth shall be blessed." (Genesis 12:1–3, ESV)

This great, blessed nation that God would make would ultimately become the people of his kingdom reign. Through this nation, all families of the earth would indeed be blessed. From Abram a great, blessed kingdom people would be born—the nation known as Israel. The nation of Israel was God's chosen people. He ruled over them as king on earth, in a way that mirrored his rule in heaven.

> For you are a people holy to the LORD your God. The LORD your God has chosen you to be a people for his treasured possession, out of all the peoples who are on the face of the earth. (Deuteronomy 7:6, ESV)

God ruled Israel and they represented that rule on earth.

> Now therefore, if you will indeed obey my voice and keep my covenant, you shall be my treasured possession among all peoples, for all the earth is mine; and you shall be to me a kingdom of priests and a holy nation. (Exodus 19:5–6, ESV)

With these words, God established a symbiotic relationship between the people and himself. The relationship rooted in God's reign over his people put on display to the earth what the kingdom life looked like.

Of course, the story continues. Israel enjoyed kingdom life—until they didn't. Their chosen status would eventually meet human resistance. Instead of being ruled *by* God, Israel sought to rule *like* God. Their desire to rule like God was never clearer than when the nation of Israel asked for a human king to judge them, just as kings ruled all the other nations. God clearly understood what was taking place and told Samuel the prophet,

"They have not rejected you, but they have rejected me from being *king* over them" (1 Samuel 8:7, ESV). This choice, however, did not come without consequences, for it began a cycle of separation and sin for Israel as the people of God.

We can see a few bright spots on the timeline of the kingdom of Israel, noted by monarchs who did what was right in the sight of God. The most notable was King David. Of course, David was not without major flaws, but he was a king who had a heart that was likened to God's. And it was to David that God promised to establish a kingdom forever (2 Samuel 7:13–16). Ironically, this promise—combined with the continued rebellion of the people, their allegiance to their own rule, and the subsequent penalty for their actions—brought about the hope of a figure who would ultimately deliver them from the oppression and separation that the sin of self-rule had brought upon them.

The prophet Isaiah spoke of the grim reality facing ancient Israel when he wrote, "But your iniquities have made a separation between you and your God, and your sins have hidden his face from you so that he does not hear" (Isaiah 59:2, ESV). Though the separation was prophesied, Isaiah also spoke bountifully about the coming of the One who would deal with their sin and rescue the people from captivity and separation to begin a new era of the kingdom.

Consider a few more prophecies of this coming figure:

> For to us a child is born, to us a son is given; and the government shall be upon his shoulder, and his name shall be called Wonderful Counselor, Mighty God, Everlasting Father, Prince of Peace. Of the increase of his government and of peace there will be no end, on the throne of David and over his kingdom, to establish it and to uphold it with justice and with righteousness from this time forth and forevermore. (Isaiah 9:6–7, ESV)
>
> Behold, a king will reign in righteousness, and princes will rule in justice. (Isaiah 32:1, ESV)

Biblical scholar N. T. Wright detects in the Psalms and in Ezekiel further descriptions of this great Deliverer. He sees that the Rescuer would be the manifestation of God himself. Wright contends that Psalm 145 reveals that this redeemer would come as a king.[3]

> I will extol you, my God and King, and bless your name forever and ever. . . . All your works shall give thanks to you, O Lord, and all your saints shall bless you! They shall speak of the glory of your kingdom and tell of your power, to make known to the children of man your mighty deeds,

> and the glorious splendor of your kingdom. Your kingdom is an everlasting kingdom, and your dominion endures throughout all generations. The LORD is faithful in all his words and kind in all his works. (Psalm 145:1, 10–13, ESV)

And Ezekiel describes the shepherding role of this king.

> I will rescue my flock; they shall no longer be a prey. And I will judge between sheep and sheep. And I will set up over them one shepherd, my servant David, and he shall feed them: he shall feed them and be their shepherd. And I, the LORD, will be their God, and my servant David shall be prince among them. I am the LORD; I have spoken. (Ezekiel 34:22–24, ESV)

What Wright gathers from Psalms and Ezekiel isn't just a keen observation; rather, it serves to cement a critical point for understanding the kingdom of God beyond the bounds of the Old Testament. It serves to point us to perceiving what the kingdom of God would look like within the realm of the New Testament age and beyond. But before we venture there, let's review the ground we've already covered.

From our look into Eden, we learned that the kingdom of God can indeed exist on earth as it does in heaven. Then we saw that there was a period of time in which God's rule over Israel displayed the kingdom, until the people's desire to rule like God consumed them. This decision, along with the sin that came with it, separated them from their true king. In the context of this separation, the prophets spoke of the hope that one day God would again actively rule his people. What we see in the New Testament is that God would rule and his kingdom would again be established by the Davidic line through Jesus.

THE KINGDOM OF GOD IN THE NEW TESTAMENT

If we see the concept of the kingdom of God introduced in the Old Testament Scriptures through the story of Israel, then we see it fulfilled in the life of Jesus of Nazareth in the New Testament. As we look at Jesus, it should be noted that in order to understand and define the kingdom of God, we can't divorce ourselves from the story of ancient Israel. Jesus is the grand connector of both Israel and the kingdom, for he is the fulfillment of the story of ancient Israel and the true king in the kingdom of God.

Jesus not only spoke often about the kingdom, as I mentioned, but his entire ministry focused on the kingdom. From the preparatory ministry of John the Baptist, who announced that the kingdom of heaven (synonymous with the "kingdom of God") was at hand in Matthew 3:2, to the Great Commission of Matthew 28:18–20, we see vivid examples of the divine monarchy breaking through on earth through the life of Jesus.

The Gospel of Matthew details the beginning of Jesus' earthly ministry: "From that time Jesus began to preach, saying, 'Repent, for the kingdom of heaven is at hand'" (Matthew 4:17, ESV). Then, in Matthew 4:23, we read that after Jesus called his first disciples, "he went throughout all Galilee, teaching in their synagogues and proclaiming the gospel of the kingdom, and healing every disease and every affliction among the people" (ESV). If Jesus' synagogue experience was similar to the one Luke narrated in Luke 4:16–19, then Matthew was describing the ways Jesus demonstrated in word and deed what the kingdom of God was all about.

Jesus' words help us to gain clarity on the mystery of the kingdom. They will allow us to define the kingdom of God by enabling us to connect it to something observable. He helps us transport something that might be viewed as theoretical into something tangible. In other words, Jesus helps us take something from the pages of the Bible and see how it could be lived out in everyday life. He takes something that was two-dimensional for us and makes it four-dimensional.

Jesus said:

> Pray then like this: "Our Father in heaven, hallowed be your name. Your kingdom come, your will be done, on earth as it is in heaven. (Matthew 6:9–10, ESV)
>
> But seek first the kingdom of God and his righteousness, and all these things will be added to you. (Matthew 6:33, ESV)
>
> Not everyone who says to me, 'Lord, Lord,' will enter the kingdom of heaven, but the one who does the will of my Father who is in heaven. (Matthew 7:21, ESV)

To illustrate this movement from "theoretical to tangible," allow me to diagram two of these texts. Matthew 6:10a says, "Your kingdom come, your will be done." This phrase does a lot to define what the kingdom of God meant to Jesus. The word *kingdom* in these texts is the Greek word *basileia*, which means "realm" or "rule." For Jesus, the kingdom was the realm where God's will would be done.

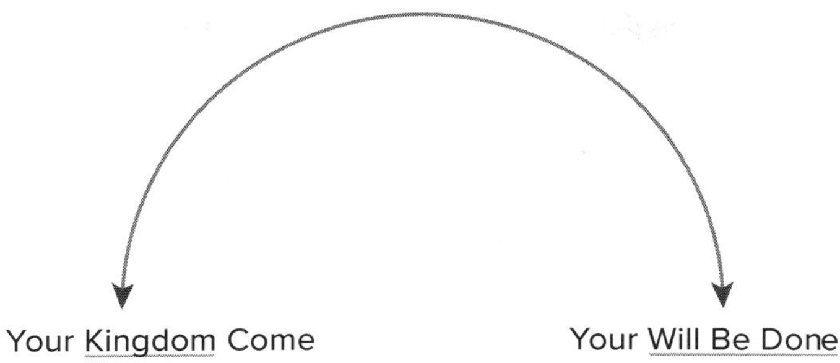

Where would this take place?

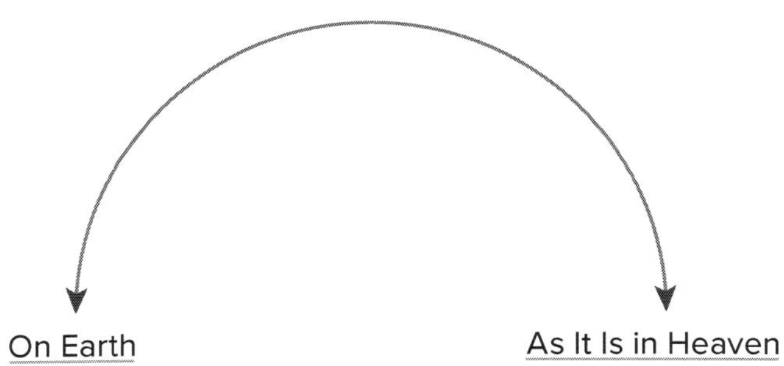

Now, let's look at Matthew 6:33 again. Here, Jesus says to "seek first the kingdom of God and his righteousness" (ESV). Within this imperative, we find a way to see the kingdom of God on earth. The righteousness of God that mankind is to seek comes through obedient and faithful behavior, which ultimately models the life of Jesus.

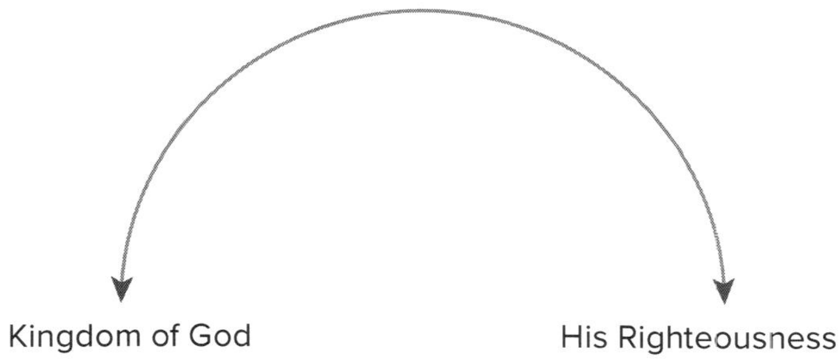

When we look at all these Scriptures combined, we see that the kingdom is the realm where the righteous will of God is being done on earth as it is in heaven.

As Matthew 4:23 indicates, whenever Jesus came into a town, he brought the message and manifestation that God's righteous will was being done on earth as it was in heaven. Not just through words but also through actions. We see the emphatic stamp of this rule over brokenness on Calvary. Jesus overcame all demonic powers, and the fate of the ruler of this world—Satan— was finally sealed at his hands (and feet) when he was crucified.

Jesus' death brought forgiveness and deliverance, not just from a salvation perspective, but from an end times perspective. It symbolized deliverance from Israel's exile and from the separation of a nation from its God. The cross extended beyond the borders of Israel and brought fulfillment to something uttered to Abraham centuries before—that in Abraham (through his seed) all families of the earth would be blessed (Genesis 12:1–3). Through the life of Jesus, promises were coming true. Righteousness was reigning. Jesus was ruling.

Jesus said in Matthew 28:18, "All authority in heaven and on earth has been given to me" (ESV). In the realm where God's will was being done, Jesus had all authority. In other words, Jesus is the king of the kingdom!

PUTTING THE PIECES TOGETHER

We can begin finding the answer to the question, "What is the kingdom of God?" by putting together the pieces of Jesus' ministry and proclamations we've covered so far. In summary, the kingdom of God is the reign of God over the brokenness of humanity, through Jesus. It is God's will being done on earth as it is in heaven, through Jesus. It is the righteousness of God poured out over the world that he created, taking place through Jesus. Karl Barth said, "The kingdom of God was more or less God ruling."[4] I would agree with Barth; however, I think it is important to add that it is God ruling *through Jesus* and that the kingdom brings the joy, peace, righteousness, and deliverance that would come through such a Messianic reign.

God's kingdom exists on the earth, but at the same time, his kingdom won't be fully consummated until eternity dawns. It is a present and eternal kingdom at the same time. In either case, Jesus is on the throne.

As George Eldon Ladd states,

> Fundamentally, as we have seen, the Kingdom of God is God's sovereign reign; but God's reign expresses itself in different stages throughout redemptive history. Therefore, men may enter into the realm of God's reign in several stages of manifestation and experience the blessings of His reign in differing degrees. God's Kingdom is the realm of the Age to Come, popularly called heaven; then we shall realize the blessings of His Kingdom (reign) in the perfection of their fullness. But the Kingdom is here now. There is a realm of spiritual blessing into which we may enter today and enjoy in part in reality the blessings of God's Kingdom (reign).[5]

This reign affects our lives when our hearts are surrendered to the kingship of Jesus. This surrender brings peace, righteousness, and deliverance into the life of the believer. When this happens, the old way of existence is buried, and a new life is born. This kingdom reign begins when we surrender to God in baptism (see Acts 2:14–41).

This reign is at the heart of what it means to be disciples of Jesus. We seek God's kingdom reign as we trust and follow Jesus as king. When we make disciples, we are gathering people into the kingdom reign of the One who has all authority, who sends us to make other disciples, and who tells us that as disciples we are to obey all of his teachings (Matthew 28:18–20). This is actually the core mission of the church on earth—to which we turn our attention to next. Specifically, the next question the book will explore is: What does the kingdom of God look like through the church?

REFLECTION & DISCUSSION QUESTIONS

1. What are some reasons that Christians have trouble understanding the kingdom of God?

2. How have you defined the kingdom of God until this point in your life? How does the chapter define the kingdom of God?

3. Are there areas of your life that you have rejected God as king?

4. Read Matthew 6:9–10. How does this passage provide clarification for you about the expansiveness of the kingdom of God?

5. Describe some of Jesus' actions during his life on earth that displayed the kingdom of God.

6. How might your inward and outward life look if you demonstrated your complete surrender to Jesus' bringing the kingdom of God to earth?

2

WHAT DOES THE KINGDOM OF GOD LOOK LIKE THROUGH THE CHURCH?

Answer: The church is an assembly of kingdom people who display the reign of God through King Jesus.

For the kingdom of God is not a matter of
eating and drinking, but of righteousness,
peace and joy in the Holy Spirit.
— Romans 14:17

Now that we have established a firm foundation of the nature of the kingdom of God in Chapter 1, we will move more quickly through the remaining chapters of this work, starting with the connection between kingdom and church. As we have discovered, the kingdom of God is a central tenet of both the Old and New Testament Scriptures, but many theologians view our next subject, the church, as a focus of the New Testament Scriptures only. Partly, as a result of this perceived reality, they view the church in lesser standing than the dynamic kingdom of God.

I contend that the church is more than we tend to make her out to be. As a matter of fact, we see God's righteous will being done on earth as it is in heaven *through the church.* The church is just as biblically meaningful as the kingdom and should be held in as high esteem.

We live in an age in which it seems popular to criticize and even disparage the church. A tremendous amount of literature has been written in recent years that speaks to what the church *isn't* doing right or how irrelevant the church is in danger of becoming. Because of such thinking, movements have sprung up in the world seeking to fulfill the role of the church, without actually being the church. Such is the case with some parachurch organizations around the world who devote themselves to doing "kingdom work."

While a case can be made for groups and organizations like these coming alongside the church—which is what the "para" in "parachurch" refers to—sometimes these organizations venture into a territory of seeking to fulfill the role of the pillar and buttress of truth (1 Timothy 3:15). Yet even with its shortcomings, the grand purpose of the church is to *reveal the kingdom.* No other grouping of people or even parachurch organization is meant to reveal God's kingdom like the church.

Disciple making—entering into relationships to help people follow Jesus, be changed by Jesus, and join the mission of Jesus—is the core work of the local church. True disciples reveal the kingdom. The local church is God's Plan A when it comes to both the kingdom and disciple making.

THE LOCAL CHURCH IS GOD'S PLAN A FOR KINGDOM AND DISCIPLE MAKING.

THE CALL TO A DIFFERENT PERSPECTIVE

TRUTHFULLY, I USED TO see things a lot differently. I would speak of "kingdom work" and associate it with many acts of service being done by people and organizations around the world. From building schools in Africa, feeding homeless people in Atlanta, or homeschooling one's kids, to me it was all "kingdom work." The idea behind my broad use of the phrase was that doing good works was clearly showing that God was reigning over an area, a city, a home, or an entire culture. Surely, it was God's will that a school be brought to an underprivileged area, right? Surely, it was God's will that the homeless were able to eat and find shelter. Surely, it was God's will that parents take a more active role in teaching their kids.

But when you consider the definition that we uncovered about the kingdom in the last chapter, simply applying the phrase "kingdom work" to a good deed doesn't quite fit. Remember, the kingdom of God is seen through God's will being done on earth as it is in heaven, *through the reign of King Jesus,* in such a way that brings peace, righteousness, and deliverance—now and in the age to come.

Good works might indeed display God's will being done, but it isn't always necessarily done through the reign of King Jesus. And though it might bring some peace, it isn't bringing the peace that King Jesus brings nor his righteousness, let alone his deliverance. Since the kingdom of God is a biblical idea, we must look to the Bible to see how this was carried out. When we do, we discover that there is only one grouping of people who ever truly lived this out through the reign of King Jesus—the church!

There are many scholars who have gone through great pains to elaborate on the idea that the kingdom and the church are different. Indeed, they are different, but they are closer than many might make them out to be. On the other hand, others seem to insinuate that the kingdom and church are synonymous. They are close, but not *that* close.

KINGDOM AND CHURCH

The kingdom of God speaks of the reign and rule of God. As I mentioned, "kingdom" is the Greek word *basileia*. The word "church" that we read in the New Testament is the word *ekklēsia* (Greek), which is connected to the Hebrew word *qahal*. These words speak of the idea of a public gathering or assembly. In the Greco-Roman world, the word went beyond just a public gathering and into the area of politics. "The *ekklēsia* was a governing council that established policies, legislated, conferred or denied citizenship, and elected officials. The *ekklēsia* had ruling powers. Don't let this fact escape you. It is the very basis of Jesus using this word."[6] The idea of a governing or ruling council is not only important for the sake of etymology, but for us understanding the purpose of the *ekklēsia*.

Jesus spoke of the *ekklēsia* in Matthew 16:15–19, where he connected it with his kingdom. In the mind of

Jesus, there was no church (*ekklēsia*) without the kingdom, and there wouldn't be a visible demonstration of the kingdom without the church. Here is what he says:

> "But who do you say that I am?" Simon Peter replied, "You are the Christ, the Son of the living God." And Jesus answered him, "Blessed are you, Simon Bar-Jonah! For flesh and blood has not revealed this to you, but my Father who is in heaven. And I tell you, you are Peter, and on this rock I will build my *church* [*ekklēsia*], and the gates of hell shall not prevail against it. I will give you the keys of the *kingdom* [*basileia*] of heaven, and whatever you bind on earth shall be bound in heaven, and whatever you loose on earth shall be loosed in heaven." (Matthew 16:15–19, ESV)

Peter's confession was "You are the Christ"—that Jesus was king! Upon hearing this, Jesus declared that Peter was blessed, for such knowledge didn't come from human teaching but from God himself. This led to another declaration by Jesus that the reality of such a rock-solid statement—that Jesus was king—would be the foundation of the church he was building. Let's make sure we grasp Peter's confession. Upon the conviction that he was king, Jesus was going to establish his people, the church. The church would be the people of

King Jesus. The *people* of a king are the human representation of his kingdom rule.

Then Jesus said that he would give Peter the keys to the kingdom of heaven. On the foundation of his kingship—the truth which Peter spoke—Jesus would build his church. That is, Jesus' kingdom would be the bedrock of the church's growth and expansion. Because Jesus said he would give the keys to Peter—the rest of the apostles and every disciple from every generation—would have the authority to open the doors of the kingdom. This would be the role of the assembly of Christ followers: to speak and live out that Jesus is king, and in so doing, open the door for men and women of any age to be ruled by him as well.

The words of the apostles, particularly Peter, opened the majestic doors of his rule in a fresh way on the day of Pentecost in Acts 2. The gospel-saturated message, combined with a powerful and visible manifestation of the Holy Spirit, enabled about three thousand souls to accept an invitation to enter into the kingdom of God. This acceptance happened through their faith expressed by repentance and baptism. Through these acts of surrender, they became the very people about whom Jesus spoke to Peter in Matthew 16—the church.

Those who heard Peter that Pentecost day were engaged in a full and complete transference from one kingdom to another. The apostle Paul explains this transference to the church in Colossae, "He has delivered us from the domain of darkness and transferred us to the kingdom of his beloved Son, in whom we have redemption, the forgiveness of sins (Colossians 1:13–14, ESV). The church is composed of those who have made the transition into the kingdom of God.

A FOREVER PEOPLE

To FURTHER UNDERSTAND THIS kingdom-church dynamic, let's look now at the message in Matthew 16 between where Jesus announced the building of his church and his declaration about the giving of the keys of the kingdom. At the end of Matthew 16:18, Jesus said the "gates of hell shall not prevail against it" (ESV)—"it" being the people of the kingdom, or the church. The word for "prevail" here means to overcome or become the dominant force over another. By saying that the gates of hell or "hades" wouldn't prevail, Jesus was saying that the powers of death and darkness wouldn't dominate the kingdom. In other words, the powers of satanic opposition would not be enough to destroy this kingdom or cause its demise. The church, then, would be a forever people of a forever kingdom of light.

The church puts on display the liberating effects of the kingdom of God for the world to see. Ancient Israel once held this role, as detailed in the previous chapter.

The church is the fulfillment of the vision of God's people in Isaiah 61:1 ("freedom for the captives and release from darkness for the prisoners"), whom the king has liberated, beyond the boundaries of ancient Israel. As Scot McKnight explains, "The church is Israel expanded."[7]

By the faith expressed in repentance and baptism, the church has gained not only the forgiveness of sins but also a return from the spiritual exile that came because of such rebellion. Ancient Israel had truly been in exile and were suffering from their plight, even until the day of Pentecost in Acts 2. Yet when the three thousand converts heard the words of the gospel of the kingdom, repented, and were baptized, they were forgiven of their sins and released from the bondage that had begun with their ancestors. This return wasn't physical, for they still remained under Roman rule, but it was spiritual and real, nonetheless. How? They were delivered from the domain of darkness of sin and death, which is the deepest liberation a human can experience.

The nation of Israel that we read about in Acts 2 and every subsequent people group after them would be invited to experience the blessings of the Great Jubilee. The Great Jubilee (or year of jubilation) was first described in Leviticus 25:8–12 as a joyous year of canceled debt and returned property.

> You shall count seven weeks of years, seven times seven years, so that the time of the seven weeks of years shall give you forty-nine years. Then you shall sound the loud trumpet on the tenth day of the seventh month. On the Day of Atonement you shall sound the trumpet throughout all your land. And you shall consecrate the fiftieth year, and proclaim liberty throughout the land to all its inhabitants. It shall be a jubilee for you, when each of you shall return to his property and each of you shall return to his clan. That fiftieth year shall be a jubilee for you; in it you shall neither sow nor reap what grows of itself nor gather the grapes from the undressed vines. For it is a jubilee. It shall be holy to you. You may eat the produce of the field. (ESV)

When Jesus described the liberation that his ministry would bring in Luke 14:18–19, King Jesus was announcing that the Great Jubilee had come again. We see the fulfillment of that jubilee in Acts 2. The church is—in a sense—the "Jubileed people!"

Since then, those of us in the church have issued an invitation to the world to enjoy the great freedom and deliverance they experience in the kingdom of God. We are ambassadors of freedom. We show the universe what the reign of God through King Jesus looks like.

We invite them to be transferred from the kingdom of self-rule into the kingdom of light.

This is Peter's point when he writes,

> But you are a chosen race, a royal priesthood, a holy nation, a people for his own possession, that you may proclaim the excellencies of him who called you out of darkness into his marvelous light. Once you were not a people, but now you are God's people; once you had not received mercy, but now you have received mercy. (1 Peter 2:9–10, ESV)

Christians are a priesthood of the kingdom who seek to announce the excellencies of the kingdom and the king. Such Christians make up the church.

The church manifests the kingdom of God through true disciples. It is vitally important to form our understanding of disciples as those people who demonstrate the kingdom reign of Jesus. Disciples advance this kingdom reign in the church by carrying out God's mission in the world.

THE CHURCH MANIFESTS THE KINGDOM OF GOD THROUGH TRUE DISCIPLES.

While Peter puts a bow on the question of how the kingdom is seen through the church, by showing us the purpose of the church, he also brings up something that we must not miss: the holiness of God's people. Holiness is a paramount subject when it comes to kingdom living, and it begs further exploration.

REFLECTION & DISCUSSION QUESTIONS

1. How is your church manifesting the kingdom of God?

2. Prior to reading this chapter, what was your understanding of the core mission of the church?

3. Based on Matthew 16:15–19, what is the rock upon which Jesus would build his church?

4. This chapter explains how every disciple of Jesus has keys to the kingdom, in a sense. How might this play out in your life?

5. What does it mean that God's people are delivered from spiritual exile?

6. As followers of Jesus, we are transferred from the kingdom of self-rule to the kingdom of light. What are some ways in which that change of kingdoms has become manifest in your life?

3

WHAT IS HOLINESS AND WHY IS IT IMPORTANT?

***Answer:** Holiness is a lifestyle of separation from self-rule to kingdom-rule. It is important because holiness reveals a people dedicated to God. Holiness is a marker of kingdom life.*

But just as he who called you is holy, so be holy in all you do; for it is written: "Be holy, because I am holy."
— 1 Peter 1:15–16

To the first-century church, the apostle Peter wrote a series of letters of instruction and exhortation. We know them as 1 Peter and 2 Peter. In the first of these letters, Peter taught the scattered and persecuted Christians in his audience about the importance of holiness. For them and for us, holiness is part of the kingdom lifestyle.

Peter sets the thematic tone early in this epistle when he instructs these pilgrims not to be conformed to the passions of their former ignorance, but "as he who called you is holy, you also be holy in all your conduct, since it is written, 'You shall be holy, for I am holy'" (1 Peter 1:15, ESV). As I mentioned already, their former ignorance came from the former kingdom under which they once lived—the kingdom of darkness. Now, however, they were to demonstrate behavior befitting the kingdom of light.

Statements such as "you shall be holy, for I am holy" are often quoted within the realm of the church, but they sometimes seem to lack the real power of expectation, which is nonetheless placed upon anyone who hears such words. This statement feels so quotable to us, but when Peter wrote it, he did it with the expectation that the church would regard it under the full weight of divine inspiration.

Yet it is difficult for us *to be holy*, largely because we don't have a sense of what it takes to accomplish this state of being. Thankfully, the New Testament writers go into much detail in order to give believers a sense of what it takes to live out our holiness in the world (e.g., 1 Peter 1:13–25; Romans 12; Hebrews 12). They took the time, not just to inform readers that God desires holiness, but also to explain what holiness looks like and how to live it out. We will delve into this, but before we listen to Peter explain the *how* of holiness, let's hear him explain the *why* behind his call to holiness. Since Peter was one of those Spirit-inspired authors and the one who revealed the issue, we can lean on him to show us the way of holiness.

HOLINESS AS SEPARATION

The word "holy" comes from the Greek word *hagios*, which uniquely expresses the idea of being separate. There was no God like Yahweh, no kingdom like his kingdom, and no people like his people. As God is separate, so his people are called to be separate. For both God and humanity, behavior and conduct reflect separateness. Holiness is a lifestyle of separation from self-rule to kingdom-rule. This is important because our lifestyle of holiness displays that the kingdom has invaded our lives.

Let's face it: life can be challenging. It often throws us circumstances and situations that tempt us to be anything but holy. Peter intimates that we as kingdom people will constantly feel a pull back into the darkness from which we came in 1 Peter 1:14: "Do not be conformed to the passions of your former ignorance" (ESV). Since that is the case, Christ-followers must distance themselves from the way they lived before they surrendered to Jesus. We must intentionally choose the holy life over our old life, distinguishing between the light and the dark. In 1 Peter 2:11–16, Peter delves into the importance of a distinctly holy life and how to live it.

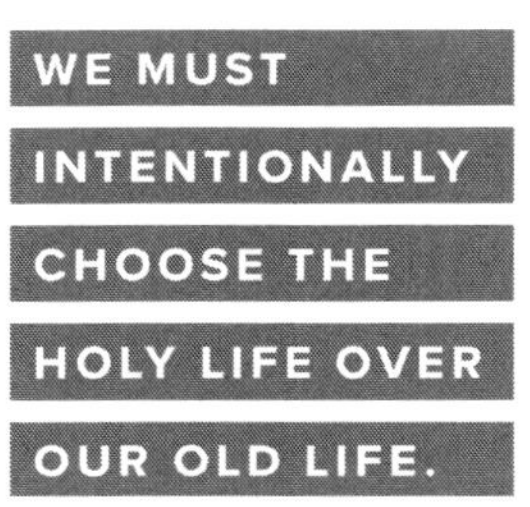

> Beloved, I urge you as sojourners and exiles to abstain from the passions of the flesh, which wage war against your soul. Keep your conduct among the Gentiles honorable, so that when they speak against you as evildoers, they may see your good deeds and glorify God on the day of visitation. (1 Peter 2:11–12, ESV)

Peter begins this instructive list by urging Christians to distance themselves from the passions and cravings of the flesh that war against their souls. When we read a phrase like "passions of the flesh," it is easy to think of it as resting solely in the realm of the sexual appetite.

However, Peter is referring to *any* fleshly or worldly behavior. He urges us against any hedonistic, self-seeking tendency that characterizes the pre-Christian, pre-church, pre-kingdom lifestyle.

As Peter explains in 1 Peter 4:2, Christians should not "live the rest of their earthly lives for evil human desires, but rather for the will of God." In other words, once we surrender to Christ, we must live not for our own will, but for the kingdom.

Such a radical approach is necessary because the kingdom life is often a life of resistance. Notice how Peter describes his audience in 1 Peter 2:11: "foreigners" and "exiles." In other words, kingdom people really aren't from "around these parts," as it were. We are citizens of heaven (Philippians 3:20). We are foreigners on enemy soil, and although we strive to love everyone genuinely and sacrificially, we stand in contradiction to the culture of the land.

After Peter tells Christ-followers about the importance of our separation from our old lives, he speaks about the seriousness of living out our holiness in front of those who are still stuck in the old way of life from which we were delivered. This "live-out-loud" quality was supposed to be seen as honorable among the unbelievers of the day, whom Peter calls "pagans." When the pagans speak evil against them (notice I said *when* not *if*), Peter says their conduct is to be such that pagans might see their good deeds and glorify God as a result: "Keep your conduct among the Gentiles honorable, so that when they speak against you as evildoers, they may see your good deeds and glorify God on the day of visitation" (1 Peter 2:12, ESV).

Peter believed that a holy lifestyle characterized by good works would counteract the slanderous words of the ancient society. The good deeds the church would do would invite others to see God. The same principle applies to the church and the world today: keep doing good and invite others to see God through those actions. After all, the church was created for good works (Ephesians 2:10) and to represent the kingdom of God to the world.

Peter writes that God would be glorified from these good deeds on the "day of visitation (1 Peter 2:12)." The "day of visitation" is either the day Jesus returns or a future conversion of some sort. I believe the latter, for we do the works of a holy priesthood so that mankind might know and obey Jesus before he returns.

Peter continues with his explanation of how to live this holy life by stating that Christians are to be subject to every human institution, whether governors or Caesar himself, as he wrote: "Be subject for the Lord's sake to every human institution, whether it be to the emperor as supreme, or to governors as sent by him to punish those who do evil and to praise those who do good

(1 Peter 2:13–14, ESV)." This would have been a difficult command because the church was being persecuted in large part by the very government he told them to subject themselves to.

It is important to note that the church isn't a collection of anarchists. The church comprises citizens of a different kingdom. They don't seek to overthrow the current government; instead, they seek to win people over to a better one. They don't do that by rabble rousing; they do it only by serving. They do it by persistently serving King Jesus.

THE IRONY OF HOLINESS

Seeking to live this type of holy lifestyle pleases our king but seeking to do so on one's own power leads only to our failure, disappointment, and discouragement. It isn't possible to live a holy existence *unless* we lean on King Jesus. As a matter of fact, allow me to say it more emphatically: we cannot live a holy life without Jesus. He is our model of holiness, and he is our advocate when we fail. His life shows us how to succeed in living the holy life, while his sacrificial death testifies to our failings and desperate need for him. The "Holy One of God" (John 6:69) is

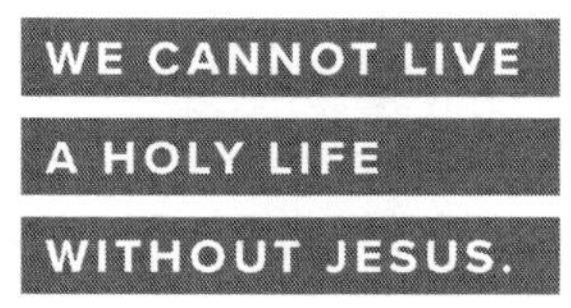

also the “Lamb of God, who takes away the sin of the world” (John 1:29).

Because of Jesus, we can live a holy, abundant life (John 10:10). Anyone can have that if they are willing to leave the kingdom of darkness for where God wants them to be—his kingdom of light. As a result, making difficult lifestyle choices becomes easier, and those choices that seem impossible become possible when we follow the pattern already set in place by King Jesus.

The life of Christ is our pattern for holiness, and our holiness is lived out each day through love.

REFLECTION & DISCUSSION QUESTIONS

1. Read 1 Peter 1:15. Is this really doable? How?

2. If holiness is a lifestyle of separation from self-rule to kingdom-rule, what are some ways this concept might apply to modern-day believers?

3. Why did Peter tell the early Christians, "Keep your conduct among the Gentiles honorable" (1 Peter 2:12, ESV)? How can you apply this in your context today?

4. Why is it important for disciples of Jesus to stand in contradiction to the culture of the land? What is at stake if we don't?

5. The early church sought to win people to the kingdom, not by violence, but by service to the kingdom. What would that look like today?

6. What areas of your life still need to transfer fully from self-rule to kingdom-rule?

4

WHAT IS LOVE AND WHY IS IT IMPORTANT?

Answer: Love is a cross-shaped action that glorifies God and benefits someone else. It is important because it is the action that best models King Jesus.

A new command I give you: Love one another. As I have loved you, so you must love one another. By this everyone will know that you are my disciples, if you love one another.
— John 13:34–35

What is love? As tempted as I am to begin singing a song by musical artist Haddaway, I will refrain. Music like that can be a wonderful window into the difficulty of answering a question like this, even as pop culture will give us mixed and even false messages about love. What is love? We *must* answer this question well if we are to live bountifully in the kingdom.

I performed a recent Google search: "How many songs are about love?" The inquiry brought up a number of websites and articles, but the first one was an article by Martin Chilton called "Deconstructing the Love Song: How and Why Love Songs Work."[8] Chilton's article estimates more than 100 million love songs have been recorded in music history. I'll let that sink in a minute: *100 million*! The interesting thing, however, is that even though the same subject has been covered over and over in music, much of the music continues to struggle with what Leonard Cohen described as "the search for the exactly right language to describe the interior landscape."[9] Chilton also quotes author and Grammy Award winner Jimmy Webb, who said, "Love is an overused word, which coincidently doesn't rhyme well with anything else."[10]

So according to Chilton and others, love is difficult to universally define, yet we use it all the time as if everyone has a shared understanding of its meaning. In our society, two people can say, "I love you," to one another and mean totally different things. What on the outside sounds like beautiful words can end up being confusing and even destructive due to our failure to accurately settle on the language that would cement its definition.

With a myriad of definitions to choose from, how do we as disciples of Jesus settle on one that befits the lifestyle of our king? First, we must detach our definition from the world that seems to hold this word hostage to its relativistic and self-centered thinking. Then, we must look at how our king defines it. Jesus is our example, and the Bible is our source for this definition.

A KINGDOM-CENTERED DEFINITION OF LOVE

The first time Jesus used the word "love" in the Gospels was during his Sermon on the Mount.

> You have heard that it was said, "You shall love your neighbor and hate your enemy." But I say to you, love your enemies and pray for those who persecute you, so that you may be sons of your Father who is in heaven. For he makes his sun rise on the evil and on the good, and sends rain on the just and on the unjust. For if you love those who love you, what reward do you have? Do not even the tax collectors do the same? And if you greet only your brothers, what more are you doing than others? Do not even the Gentiles do the same? You

> therefore must be perfect, as your heavenly Father is perfect. (Matthew 5:43–48, ESV)

The word Jesus used for "love" is the Greek word *agapaō*, which is the verb form of the noun, *agapē*. These words suggest the unconditional love with which God himself loves. This is the highest level of love possible. The verb connotes the act of demonstrating, rather than being simply a feeling. When Jesus spoke of love, he wasn't referring to a fuzzy and warm feeling that someone has for their neighbor; he spoke of an action that is demonstrated toward them. But what type of action?

Jesus began to answer this question in John 3:16 when he said that love was displayed through the action of the Father's sending his only Son. This process would deliver eternal life to those who believed in him. It was ultimately this action of sacrifice that Jesus called his disciples to as he commanded them to love their enemies and pray for those who persecuted them. To follow through on these commands, his disciples would have to absorb pain, while someone else received the immediate benefit. By loving in this way, they would be in alignment with how God loves, for love mimics God. Love is an action that benefits another, even when it might cause our pain.

LOVE BENEFITS ANOTHER, EVEN WHEN IT MIGHT CAUSE OUR PAIN.

We again see a focus on this *agapaō* love in what is often called the Greatest Commandment passage. A scribe asked Jesus which was the greatest commandment. To which, Jesus answered:

> The most important is, "Hear, O Israel: The Lord our God, the Lord is one. And you shall love the Lord your God with all your heart and with all your soul and with all your mind and with all your strength." The second is this: "You shall love your neighbor as yourself." There is no other commandment greater than these. (Mark 12:29–31, ESV)

Jesus quoted a Hebrew prayer here, often known as the *Shema*. He illustrated the prioritization of loving God with everything that makes you *you*. It is an "all of me" type of love that extends upward to God and outward to the neighbor. It kindles worship and obedience; it cultivates consideration and care; and it ignites praise of God that fuels affection for others.

Love moves up and out. If I gave you a pen and paper and asked you to draw a line upward and a line outward with both lines intersecting one another, the shape you would end up creating would be a cross! And that is the picture of love. *Love is cross-shaped.*

LOVE MOVES UP AND OUT.

Jesus' death on a Roman cross was the full demonstration of love. It was upward—in that it was in full obedience to the Father's will—and it was outward—in that it was for the salvation of all mankind. It was a self-denying sacrifice that pleased the Father and helped others. What he did on that old, rugged cross was for God's glory and for our benefit. It brought us gain, while it brought him pain. "Greater love has no one than this, that someone lay down his life for his friends" (John 15:13, ESV).

So, with all of this being said, we can define love like this:

Love is a cross-shaped action that glorifies God and benefits someone else.

This cross-shaped action must influence the life of those seeking to be his disciples. As a matter of fact, this type of love is the hallmark of one who walks as a disciple of Jesus.

> A new command I give you: Love one another. As I have loved you, so you must love one another. By this everyone will know that you are my disciples, if you love one another. (John 13:34–35)

Everyone will recognize the disciple of Jesus by the way they show love. Disciples commit to loving this way because they have committed themselves to Jesus. It is partly what makes the disciple and this cross-shaped level of love uncommon.

I DON'T SEE IT

We do not commonly see love like this in the world today. We see the love of country, the love of a political party, and the love of freedom touted on political ads and evening news programs. But these forms of love-defining advertisements usually all come with boundaries or limitations. If I love my country and my political party, then that often means I must vehemently and negatively oppose those on the other side of the aisle, who—of course—want to "ruin" the country. The kingdom of darkness says if I love one group of people, then there is another group I must hate. The kingdom of God, however, says true love knows no bounds.

This non-cross-shaped "love" that characterizes the world's love too often attaches itself to the church under the radar. And when it does, it is destructive. Always. *HuffPost* contributor Hillary Adler penned a tragic plea to Christians from her now ex-Christian perspective. She writes in her article "The Ugly in Christianity":

> I proudly called myself a Christian. Now I shy away from the term. I avoid discussions about it because I have family members I love so much

> who are still part of the Church. But, I will never again be one of them. And I'll tell you why: when I was 18, a freshman in college, on the cusp of adulthood, already questioning my faith and whether or not I even believed in organized religion, a woman stood up in a Wednesday Bible class and said, "Praise the Lord! Ted Kennedy is dead!" I sat there slack-jawed, shocked, and disgusted, and the dimming light to my already fragile faith flickered out as everybody in the room—even an elder—laughed.

You get the idea that she's dismayed by this experience. Then, she continues and ties her experience to love (or lack thereof).

> They laughed and laughed, and the woman said, "If I could, I'd go dance on his grave." She did a little jig and turned around with her hands in the air and again, once again, there was more laughter. Louder laughter. I wish I could say that was an isolated event. But things like that happened often. They happened and nobody stopped them, and judging by Facebook comments, I'm pretty sure they probably continue today.
>
> The truth is, that kind of attitude cannot coexist with God in any form. I loved that church dearly,

> I truly did. But at some point, I learned that the love of the Church only extended to the end of its borders, to the end of the doors. Outside those doors, there was very little love to give.[11]

Our hearts break for Hillary—and not only for her but for everyone she represents.[12] Hillary represents those who expected the supernatural love of the New Testament in the church but were left feeling bitterly disappointed.

Remember, the church is an assembly of kingdom people, who are set apart to live holy lives for our king. This is a loving kind of life—a life spent showing the love that points to God and blesses others. While stories like Hillary's are much too common, this can change. And since stories like this happen, we know that the church isn't always fulfilling its mandate to be kingdom people upon this earth. This needs to change—this must change. In the next chapter, I explore how we can change, beginning today.

REFLECTION & DISCUSSION QUESTIONS

1. How is this chapter's definition of love different from how the world defines love?

2. Give specific examples of Jesus showing love to others in the Bible.

3. The words Jesus uses for "love"—*agapaō* and *agapē*—connote unconditional love. Why would Jesus command us to cultivate unconditional love?

4. Read the command in Mark 12:28–31. Describe the love that we are to show to God.

5. Give examples of how you can love both upward and outward at the same time.

6. In what ways do you die to self when you disciple others through the love of Jesus?

5

HOW DOES THE CHURCH EXPRESS LOVE TO THE WORLD?

Answer: By letting love rule over all she does.

Therefore, as we have opportunity, let us
do good to all people, especially to those
who belong to the family of believers.
— Galatians 6:10

When I first got started in ministry, I was blessed to serve as a youth minister. I thoroughly enjoyed helping shape the spiritual lives of young people. We ran a children's worship program during the main gathering of the congregation that I served, in which we assembled children ages four to eleven in a separate part of the church building. We enjoyed a time of worship, praise, and instruction in a way all the kids could understand.

As part of the program, we had several rules, one of them being that parents had to check their kids into the kids' area by 10:30 a.m. This gave a few minutes of late-arriving "grace," since our main assembly started at 10:15 a.m. We established this check-in time because the space we used was extremely small and could only accommodate a certain number of kids. We also didn't want this time of worship to serve as a babysitting service for overactive children who had begun distracting their parents in the adult service. We really sought to point these kids to God during that time. With that being the case, I thought this rule was reasonable and figured everyone else felt the same way—until one Sunday morning.

A father brought his daughter around 10:45 a.m. and wanted me to admit her into our program. I informed him that we were unable to accommodate her, as we had passed the period of admittance. He was indignant: "What do you mean she can't come?"

Not wanting to cause a scene in the middle of the hallway at church, I said, "I'm sorry, that's our rule." Then I went on to explain the rationale behind it. I thought that would be good enough, but it wasn't.

He responded, "Rules?! What do you mean *rules*?"

What alarmed me wasn't so much *what* he said or even *how* he said it; it was the look on his face when he did. He seriously looked as if he were ready to punch me in the mouth and admit his daughter himself, so he could go back into the main assembly and resume praising God! I am glad to say that he didn't do any of that. Instead, he stormed off with his daughter, shaking his head, and uttering something about "rules" under his breath.

WE DON'T LIKE RULES: NO MATTER WHO MAKES THEM

People naturally resist rules. They confine us with boundaries, and people don't like feeling confined. Rules tell us what to do, but we don't like being told what to do—by anyone! People start wars over rules. We respond in rebellion because of rules. And youth ministers almost get punched in the face because of rules. People do not like rules!

Without rules, however, people experience chaos. Just as people start wars because of rules, wars also begin *in the absence of rules.* Even the person who hates rules will be forced to admit eventually that we need them. They help us make sense of things and get things done. In a sense, universal rules . . . rule.

For the church, love is the rule of life. It is *the* rule, and it rules over everything we do. For the church, love is a noun and a verb, and it must be treated as such at all times. It guides behavior, conversations, and attitudes. It governs how we operate, even when people are "breaking the rule" and not showing love toward us.

LOVE IS THE RULE OF LIFE.

LOVE RULES

Jesus firmly established "the rule" of love in a conversation with his disciples, in the sense of how he expected them to love one another: "A new command I give you: Love one another. As I have loved you, so you must love one another. By this everyone will know that you are my disciples, if you love one another" (John 13:34–35). Again, the command to love wasn't a new commandment, for we see love demonstrated throughout the Old Testament. The disciples were already familiar with love. What Jesus put forward here is not the introduction of what love is, but rather a new standard of how to love that is to characterize his disciples.

He charged them to love one another, the way in which he himself loved them. Jesus' love, as seen through laying down his life for his friends, displayed his allegiance to God and was done for the benefit of others. This type of love would be the billboard of their identity as disciples. This was his *rule* of love.

The church is full of disciples of Jesus and, as such, we are all held to his standard of loving. The rule we must live by is this: Love each other the way Jesus loves us. That love asks us to lift others up even if we might suffer in the process. This expression of sacrificial love surprises the world around us and allows them to see who we are truly.

LOVE *ACTUALLY*

We see the principles of love written by a variety of biblical writers, but I am going to focus on what many call the "love chapter," also known as 1 Corinthians 13. I have seen that whether someone is "churched" or "unchurched," this section of Scripture is referred to in many weddings as a rule of how people should love one another. Paul writes:

> Love is patient, love is kind. It does not envy,
> it does not boast, it is not proud. It does not
> dishonor others, it is not self-seeking, it is not easily
> angered, it keeps no record of wrongs. Love does

> not delight in evil but rejoices with the truth. It always protects, always trusts, always hopes, always perseveres. (1 Corinthians 13:4–7)

These verses reveal Paul's vision of how the church must display love to one another, and even to the world. Love must be even-tempered and gentle. It propels us to rejoice in the good that someone else has. Love causes us to humble ourselves and elevate someone else's needs or wants ahead of our own. It doesn't fly off the handle or keep score of someone's mistakes. If I truly love someone, I don't rejoice in their wrongdoing; instead, I find my delight in the truth. With love, I endure whatever comes up. I strive to think the best of someone, and I work to see the brighter side.

Cross-shaped love is the fuel that drives disciple making. It is the passion behind the church's highest priority. It is the key foundational motivation for all who want to love people and make disciples the way Jesus made disciples.

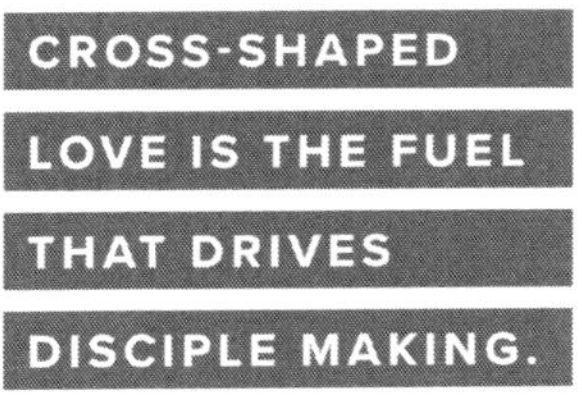

We all want this type of love too. Men, women, boys, and girls—we all crave this love. Truth be told, our lives rarely feel complete unless we experience some semblance of God's love. And the church is the Christ-centered community where everyone who needs it can find it—all because the church is living under the rule of love.

This love should stand out because people in the world typically live angry, reactive, and self-centered lives. One might say that the world has always been this way, but I think we can agree that the advent of social media has taken things to a whole new level. If we post something someone doesn't like, that person can let the world know in real time about their anger. When they disagree, instead of simply voicing their opinion, they cancel the other, unfriend them, or rant against them.

All of this angry, self-centered reactivity reminds us all the more that the world needs God's love. When political rivals brutally attack one another, I know that what we need is more love. When the divorce rate stays on the rise instead of decreasing, I know that we need more love. When kids and others are still being abused, kidnapped, and sold into sex slavery, I know that we need more love. When the racism of the past is still with us in the present, I know that we need more love. When injustice reigns over justice, I know that we need more love.

King Jesus knows we need more love too. Thus, he left his church here with the command: to let love rule. We have countless Scriptures that tell us this, all of which come from Jesus' command for us to love.

> Love your neighbor as yourself. (Mark 12:31, ESV)
>
> Therefore, as we have opportunity, let us do good to all people, especially to those who belong to the family of believers. (Galatians 6:10)
>
> Anyone who loves their brother and sister lives in the light, and there is nothing in them to make them stumble. (1 John 2:10)

When the church lets Jesus' love rule, we become a haven for the brokenhearted, a sanctuary for the oppressed, and a refuge for the weary. Why? Because everyone, truly everyone, is searching for the love that the church has to share. We display love when we let love rule our lives.

REFLECTION & DISCUSSION QUESTIONS

1. When you think of a "rule," does that have a positive or a negative connotation for you?

2. Love cannot be forced; otherwise, it's not really *love*. What are some examples in your life when you freely chose to love someone well, even when you didn't feel like it?

3. Against which society rules do you tend to rebel? What biblical rules do you tend to resist?

4. How does your church express Jesus' rule to love as he loved us (see John 13:34–35)?

5. Read 1 Corinthians 13:4–7. How does this description of love apply to disciple making?

6. What practical steps can you take to demonstrate love for the world as well as for those in your relationship circle?

APPENDIX A

BOOK RECOMMENDATIONS FOR FURTHER STUDY

Francis Chan, *Letters to the Church* (Colorado Springs: David C. Cook, 2019).

Tony Evans, *The Kingdom Agenda* (Chicago: Moody Publishers, 2013).

David Young, *King Jesus and the Beauty of Obedience-Based Discipleship* (Grand Rapids: Zondervan Reflective, 2020).

David Platt, *Radical Together: Unleashing the People of God for the Purpose of God* (Colorado Springs: Multnomah Books, 2011).

N. T. Wright, *How God Became King: The Forgotten Story of the Gospels* (New York: HarperOne, 2016).

APPENDIX B

RENEW.ORG NETWORK LEADERS' VALUES AND FAITH STATEMENTS

Mission: We Renew the Teachings of Jesus to Fuel Disciple Making

Vision: A collaborative network equipping millions of disciples, disciple makers, and church planters among all ethnicities.

SEVEN VALUES

Renewal in the Bible and in history follows a discernible outline that can be summarized by seven key elements. We champion these elements as our core values. They are listed in a sequential pattern that is typical of renewal, and it all starts with God.

1. *Renewing by God's Spirit.* We believe that God is the author of renewal and that he invites us to access and join him through prayer and fasting for the Holy Spirit's work of renewal.
2. *Following God's Word.* We learn the ways of God with lasting clarity and conviction by trusting God's Word and what it teaches as the objective foundation for renewal and life.
3. *Surrendering to Jesus' Lordship.* The gospel teaches us that Jesus is Messiah (King) and Lord. He calls everyone to salvation (in eternity) and discipleship (in this life) through a faith commitment that is expressed in repentance, confession, and baptism. Repentance and surrender to Jesus as Lord is the never-ending cycle for life in Jesus' kingdom, and it is empowered by the Spirit.
4. *Championing disciple making.* Jesus personally gave us his model of disciple making, which he demonstrated with his disciples. Those same principles from the life of Jesus should be utilized as we make disciples today and champion discipleship as the core mission of the local church.
5. *Loving like Jesus.* Jesus showed us the true meaning of love and taught us that sacrificial love is the

distinguishing character trait of true disciples (and true renewal). Sacrificial love is the foundation for our relationships both in the church and in the world.

6. *Living in holiness.* Just as Jesus lived differently from the world, the people in his church will learn to live differently than the world. Even when it is difficult, we show that God's kingdom is an alternative kingdom to the world.
7. *Leading courageously.* God always uses leaders in renewal who live by a prayerful, risk-taking faith. Renewal will be led by bold and courageous leaders—who make disciples, plant churches, and create disciple making movements.

TEN FAITH STATEMENTS

We believe that Jesus Christ is Lord. We are a group of church leaders inviting others to join the theological and disciple making journey described below. We want to trust and follow Jesus Christ to the glory of God the Father in the power of the Holy Spirit. We are committed to *restoring* the kingdom vision of Jesus and the apostles, especially the *message* of Jesus' gospel, the *method* of disciple making he showed us, and the *model* of what a community of his disciples, at their best, can become.

We live in a time when cultural pressures are forcing us to face numerous difficulties and complexities in following God. Many are losing their resolve. We trust that God is gracious and forgives the errors of those with genuine faith in his Son, but our desire is to be faithful in all things.

Our focus is disciple making, which is both reaching lost people (evangelism) and bringing people to maturity (sanctification). We seek to be a movement of disciple making leaders who make disciples and other disciple makers. We want to renew existing churches and help plant multiplying churches.

1. *God's Word.* We believe God gave us the sixty-six books of the Bible to be received as the inspired, authoritative, and infallible Word of God for salvation and life. The documents of Scripture come to us as diverse literary and historical writings. Despite their complexities, they can be understood, trusted, and followed. We want to do the hard work of wrestling to understand Scripture in order to obey God. We want to avoid the errors of interpreting Scripture through the sentimental lens of our feelings and opinions or through a complex re-interpretation of plain meanings so that the Bible says what our culture says. Ours is a time for both clear thinking and courage. Because the Holy Spirit inspired all sixty-six books, we honor Jesus' Lordship by submitting our lives to all that God has for us in them.

Psalm 1; 119; Deuteronomy 4:1–6; 6:1–9; 2 Chronicles 34; Nehemiah 8; Matthew 5:1–7:28; 15:6–9; John 12:44–50; Matthew 28:19; Acts 2:42; 17:10–11; 2 Timothy 3:16–4:4; 1 Peter 1:20–21.

2. *Christian convictions.* We believe the Scriptures reveal three distinct elements of the faith: *essential* elements which are necessary for salvation; *important* elements which are to be pursued so that we faithfully follow Christ; and *personal* elements or opinion. The gospel is *essential.* Every person who is indwelt and sealed by God's Holy Spirit because of their faith in the gospel is a brother or a sister in Christ. *Important* but secondary elements of the faith are vital. Our faithfulness to God requires us to seek and pursue them, even as we acknowledge that our salvation may not be dependent on getting them right. And thirdly, there are personal matters of opinion, disputable areas where God gives us personal freedom. But we are never at liberty to express our freedom in a way that causes others to stumble in sin. In all things, we want to show understanding, kindness, and love.

1 Corinthians 15:1–8; Romans 1:15–17; Galatians 1:6–9; 2 Timothy 2:8; Ephesians 1:13–14; 4:4–6; Romans 8:9; 1 Corinthians 12:13; 1 Timothy 4:16; 2 Timothy 3:16–4:4;

Matthew 15:6–9; Acts 20:32; 1 Corinthians 11:1–2; 1 John 2:3–4; 2 Peter 3:14–16; Romans 14:1–23.

3. *The gospel.* We believe God created all things and made human beings in his image, so that we could enjoy a relationship with him and each other. But we lost our way, through Satan's influence. We are now spiritually dead, separated from God. Without his help, we gravitate toward sin and self-rule. The gospel is God's good news of reconciliation. It was promised to Abraham and David and revealed in Jesus' life, ministry, teaching, and sacrificial death on the cross. The gospel is the saving action of the triune God. The Father sent the Son into the world to take on human flesh and redeem us. Jesus came as the promised Messiah of the Old Testament. He ushered in the kingdom of God, died for our sins according to Scripture, was buried, and was raised on the third day. He defeated sin and death and ascended to heaven. He is seated at the right hand of God as Lord and he is coming back for his disciples. Through the Spirit, we are transformed and sanctified. God will raise everyone for the final judgment. Those who trusted and followed Jesus by faith will not experience punishment for their sins and separation from God in hell. Instead, we will join together with God in the renewal of all things in the consummated kingdom. We will live

together in the new heaven and new earth where we will glorify God and enjoy him forever.

Genesis 1–3; Romans 3:10–12; 7:8–25; Genesis 12:1–3; Galatians 3:6–9; Isaiah 11:1–4; 2 Samuel 7:1–16; Micah 5:2–4; Daniel 2:44–45; Luke 1:33; John 1:1–3; Matthew 4:17; 1 Corinthians 15:1–8; Acts 1:11; 2:36; 3:19–21; Colossians 3:1; Matthew 25:31–32; Revelation 21:1ff; Romans 3:21–26.

4. *Faithful faith.* We believe that people are saved by grace through faith. The gospel of Jesus' kingdom calls people to both salvation and discipleship—no exceptions, no excuses. Faith is more than mere intellectual agreement or emotional warmth toward God. It is living and active; faith is surrendering our self-rule to the rule of God through Jesus in the power of the Spirit. We surrender by trusting and following Jesus as both Savior and Lord in all things. Faith includes allegiance, loyalty, and faithfulness to him.

Ephesians 2:8–9; Mark 8:34–38; Luke 14:25–35; Romans 1:3, 5; 16:25–26; Galatians 2:20; James 2:14–26; Matthew 7:21–23; Galatians 4:19; Matthew 28:19–20; 2 Corinthians 3:3, 17–18; Colossians 1:28.

5. *New birth.* God so loved the world that he gave his one and only Son, that whoever believes in him shall not perish but have eternal life. To believe in Jesus means we trust and follow him as both Savior and Lord. When we commit to trust and follow Jesus, we express this faith by repenting from sin, confessing his name, and receiving baptism by immersion in water. Baptism, as an expression of faith, is for the remission of sins. We uphold baptism as the normative means of entry into the life of discipleship. It marks our commitment to regularly die to ourselves and rise to live for Christ in the power of the Holy Spirit. We believe God sovereignly saves as he sees fit, but we are bound by Scripture to uphold this teaching about surrendering to Jesus in faith through repentance, confession, and baptism.

1 Corinthians 8:6; John 3:1–9; 3:16–18; 3:19–21; Luke 13:3–5; 24:46–47; Acts 2:38; 3:19; 8:36–38; 16:31–33; 17:30; 20:21; 22:16; 26:20; Galatians 3:26–27; Romans 6:1–4; 10:9–10; 1 Peter 3:21; Romans 2:25–29; 2 Chronicles 30:17–19; Matthew 28:19–20; Galatians 2:20; Acts 18:24–26.

6. *Holy Spirit.* We believe God's desire is for everyone to be saved and come to the knowledge of the truth. Many hear the gospel but do not believe it because they

are blinded by Satan and resist the pull of the Holy Spirit. We encourage everyone to listen to the Word and let the Holy Spirit convict them of their sin and draw them into a relationship with God through Jesus. We believe that when we are born again and indwelt by the Holy Spirit, we are to live as people who are filled, empowered, and led by the Holy Spirit. This is how we walk with God and discern his voice. A prayerful life, rich in the Holy Spirit, is fundamental to true discipleship and living in step with the kingdom reign of Jesus. We seek to be a prayerful, Spirit-led fellowship.

1 Timothy 2:4; John 16:7–11; Acts 7:51; 1 John 2:20, 27; John 3:5; Ephesians 1:13–14; 5:18; Galatians 5:16–25; Romans 8:5–11; Acts 1:14; 2:42; 6:6; 9:40; 12:5; 13:3; 14:23; 20:36; 2 Corinthians 3:3.

7. *Disciple making.* We believe the core mission of the local church is making disciples of Jesus Christ—it is God's plan "A" to redeem the world and manifest the reign of his kingdom. We want to be disciples who make disciples because of our love for God and others. We personally seek to become more and more like Jesus through his Spirit so that Jesus would live through us. To help us focus on Jesus, his sacrifice on the cross, our unity in him, and his coming return, we typically share

communion in our weekly gatherings. We desire the fruits of biblical disciple making which are disciples who live and love like Jesus and "go" into every corner of society and to the ends of the earth. Disciple making is the engine that drives our missional service to those outside the church. We seek to be known where we live for the good that we do in our communities. We love and serve all people, as Jesus did, no strings attached. At the same time, as we do good for others, we also seek to form relational bridges that we prayerfully hope will open doors for teaching people the gospel of the kingdom and the way of salvation.

Matthew 28:19–20; Galatians 4:19;
Acts 2:41; Philippians 1:20–21; Colossians 1:27–29;
2 Corinthians 3:3; 1 Thessalonians 2:19–20;
John 13:34–35; 1 John 3:16; 1 Corinthians 13:1–13;
Luke 22:14–23; 1 Corinthians 11:17–24; Acts 20:7.

8. *Kingdom life.* We believe in the present kingdom reign of God, the power of the Holy Spirit to transform people, and the priority of the local church. God's holiness should lead our churches to reject lifestyles characterized by pride, sexual immorality, homosexuality, easy divorce, idolatry, greed, materialism, gossip, slander, racism, violence, and the like. God's love should lead our churches to emphasize love as the distinguishing sign of

a true disciple. Love for one another should make the church like an extended family—a fellowship of married people, singles, elderly, and children who are all brothers and sisters to one another. The love of the extended church family to one another is vitally important. Love should be expressed in both service to the church and to the surrounding community. It leads to the breaking down of walls (racial, social, political), evangelism, acts of mercy, compassion, forgiveness, and the like. By demonstrating the ways of Jesus, the church reveals God's kingdom reign to the watching world.

1 Corinthians 1:2; Galatians 5:19–21;
Ephesians 5:3–7; Colossians 3:5–9;
Matthew 19:3–12; Romans 1:26–32; 14:17–18;
1 Peter 1:15–16; Matthew 25:31–46;
John 13:34–35; Colossians 3:12–13; 1 John 3:16;
1 Corinthians 13:1–13; 2 Corinthians 5:16–21.

9. *Counter-cultural living.* We believe Jesus' Lordship through Scripture will lead us to be a distinct light in the world. We follow the first and second Great Commandments where love and loyalty to God come first and love for others comes second. So we prioritize the gospel and one's relationship with God, with a strong commitment to love people in their secondary points of need too. The gospel is God's light for us. It teaches us

grace, mercy, and love. It also teaches us God's holiness, justice, and the reality of hell which led to Jesus' sacrifice of atonement for us. God's light is grace and truth, mercy and righteousness, love and holiness. God's light among us should be reflected in distinctive ways like the following:

A. We believe that human life begins at conception and ends upon natural death, and that all human life is priceless in the eyes of God. All humans should be treated as image-bearers of God. For this reason, we stand for the sanctity of life both at its beginning and its end. We oppose elective abortions and euthanasia as immoral and sinful. We understand that there are very rare circumstances that may lead to difficult choices when a mother or child's life is at stake, and we prayerfully surrender and defer to God's wisdom, grace, and mercy in those circumstances.
B. We believe God created marriage as the context for the expression and enjoyment of sexual relations. Jesus defines marriage as a covenant between one man and one woman. We believe that all sexual activity outside the bounds of marriage, including same-sex unions and same-sex marriage, are immoral and must not be condoned by disciples of Jesus.

C. We believe that Jesus invites all races and ethnicities into the kingdom of God. Because humanity has exhibited grave racial injustices throughout history, we believe that everyone, especially disciples, must be proactive in securing justice for people of all races and that racial reconciliation must be a priority for the church.

D. We believe that both men and women were created by God to equally reflect, in gendered ways, the nature and character of God in the world. In marriage, husbands and wives are to submit to one another, yet there are gender specific expressions: husbands model themselves in relationship with their wives after Jesus' sacrificial love for the church, and wives model themselves in relationship with their husbands after the church's willingness to follow Jesus. In the church, men and women serve as partners in the use of their gifts in ministry, while seeking to uphold New Testament norms which teach that the lead teacher/preacher role in the gathered church and the elder/overseer role are for qualified men. The vision of the Bible is an equal partnership of men and women in creation, in marriage, in salvation, in the gifts of the Spirit, and in the ministries of the church but exercised in ways that honor gender as described in the Bible.

E. We believe that we must resist the forces of culture that focus on materialism and greed. The Bible teaches that the love of money is the root of all sorts of evil and that greed is idolatry. Disciples of Jesus should joyfully give liberally and work sacrificially for the poor, the marginalized, and the oppressed.

Romans 12:3–8; Matthew 22:36–40; 1 Corinthians 12:4–7; Ephesians 2:10; 4:11–13; 1 Peter 4:10–11; Matthew 20:24–27; Philippians 1:1; Acts 20:28; 1 Timothy 2:11–15; 3:1–7; Titus 1:5–9; 1 Corinthians 11:2–9; 14:33–36; Ephesians 5:21–33; Colossians 3:18–19; 1 Corinthians 7:32–35.

10. *The end.* We believe that Jesus is coming back to earth in order to bring this age to an end. Jesus will reward the saved and punish the wicked, and finally destroy God's last enemy, death. He will put all things under the Father, so that God may be all in all forever. That is why we have urgency for the Great Commission—to make disciples of all nations. We like to look at the Great Commission as an inherent part of God's original command to "be fruitful and multiply."

We want to be disciples of Jesus who love people and help them to be disciples of Jesus. We are a movement of disciples who make disciples who help renew existing churches and who start new churches that make more disciples. We want to reach as many as possible—until Jesus returns and God restores all creation to himself in the new heaven and new earth.

Matthew 25:31–32; Acts 17:31; Revelation 20:11–15; 2 Thessalonians 1:6–10; Mark 9:43–49; Luke 12:4–7; Acts 4:12; John 14:6; Luke 24:46–48; Matthew 28:19–20; Genesis 12:1–3; Galatians 2:20; 4:19; Luke 6:40; Luke 19:10; Revelation 21:1ff.

NOTES

1. David Young, *King Jesus and the Beauty of Obedience-Based Discipleship* (Grand Rapids: Zondervan, 2020), 18.

2. Scot McKnight, *Kingdom Conspiracy: Returning to the Radical Mission of the Local Church* (Grand Rapids: Brazos Baker, 2016), 66–73.

3. N. T. Wright, *Simply Jesus: A New Vision of Who He Was, What He Did, and Why He Matters* (New York: HarperOne, 2018), 43–56.

4. Karl Barth, *The Christian Life* (Grand Rapids: Eerdmans, 1981), 233–260.

5. George Eldon Ladd, *The Gospel of the Kingdom: Scriptural Studies in the Kingdom of God* (Grand Rapids: Eerdmans, 2011), 22.

6. Tim Kurtz, *Leaving Church Becoming Ekklesia: Because Jesus Never Said He Would Build a Church* (Alison, MI: Kingdom Word Publications, 2017), 58, Kindle.

7. Scot McKnight, *Kingdom Conspiracy: Returning to the Radical Mission of the Local Church* (Grand Rapids: Brazos Baker, 2016), 89.

8. Martin Chilton, "Deconstructing the Love Song: How and Why Love Songs Work," uDiscover Music, accessed September 10, 2020, https://www.udiscovermusic.com/in-depth-features/deconstructing-the-love-song-how-they-work/.

9. Ibid.

10. Ibid.

11. Hillary Adler, "The Ugly in Christianity," *HuffPost*, June 8, 2016, https://www.huffpost.com/entry/the-ugly-in-christianity_b_57588f08e4b053e219786f6b.

12. This response to Hillary Adler's plea to the church is well-expressed by Don McLaughlin in *Love First: Ending Hate Before It's Too Late* (Abilene: Leafwood Publishers, 2017), 28–29.

Made in the USA
Columbia, SC
24 August 2021